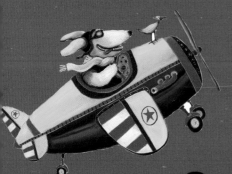

Outside of a dog, a book is man's best friend. Inside of a dog it's too dark to read.

–Groucho Marx

picturebook

Picturebook 01
Copyright 2000
Published by WaterMark, Inc.
2080 Valleydale Road
Birmingham, AL 35244
www.picture-book.com

Printed and bound in Italy
by
Bolis Poligrafiche

Cover illustration Copyright 2000 by Corey Wolfe(pp 132-133)
Spine illustration Copyright 2000 by Drew Rose (p 74)
Illustration on previous page Copyright 2000 by Lee Chapman (p 214)
and John Kovaleski (p 7)
Illustration this page Copyright 2000 by Drew Rose (p 74)
Title page illustration Copyright 2000 by Selina Alko (p 161)

ISBN 1-882077-93-8

Picturebook is an illustrator sourcebook targeted to the specific field of artwork executed for children. On page after page, some of the best illustrators in the business can be found. Finding the perfect illustrator for your next project has never been so easy!

Picturebook 01

picturebook 01

Directory of Children's Illustration

studio: **615.595.5580**

dd@dennasd.com

www.dennasd.com

Dennas Davis

Karen Malzeke-McDonald
Design and Illustration

16 FOX LANE WEST • PAINTED POST, NY 14870

PHONE/FAX

607 · 936 · 3108

E-mail karenmcd96@aol.com

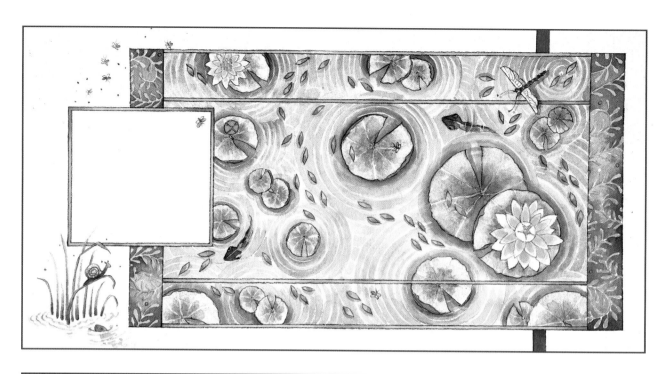

·MARY·HAVERFIELD·

PHONE·214·520·2548 FAX·214·528·3072

Melissa Turk & THE ARTIST NETWORK

PEDRO GONZALEZ

DREW-BROOK-CORMACK

DARA GOLDMAN

TIM DAVIS

KA BOTZIS

NANCY DIDION

ELIZABETH WOLF

WENDY SMITH

CLAUDIA KARABAIC SARGENT

NEECY TWINEM

BRIDGET STARR TAYLOR   JANE CHAMBLESS WRIGHT

MARY TEICHMAN

KEVIN O'MALLEY

phone (845) 368-8606 ● www.theispot.com/rep/melissaturk/

The Many Characters of Illustration . . .

ELIZABETH WOLF

Melissa Turk
THE ARTIST NETWORK

phone (845) 368-8606 / fax (845) 368-8608   9 babbling brook lane / suffern, new york 10901

www.theispot.com/rep/melissaturk/

KEVIN O'MALLEY

KA BOTZIS

12

N E E C Y T W I N E M

13

BRIDGET STARR TAYLOR

TIM DAVIS

DREW-BROOK-CORMACK

WENDY SMITH

JANE WRIGHT

MARY TEICHMAN

Melissa Turk
THE ARTIST NETWORK

phone (845) 368-8606 / fax (845) 368-8608   9 babbling brook lane / suffern, new york 10901

www.theispot.com/rep/melissaturk/

14

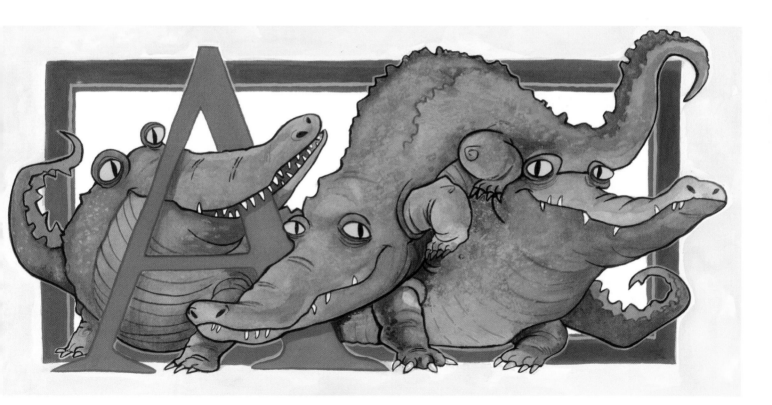

jeff shelly

www.jeffshelly.com

2330 San Marco Dr. Los Angeles, CA 90068 (800)318-3244 (323)460-4604 Fax(323)464-6630

419 22nd Avenue
San Francisco, CA 94121
415.668.7156
email: ppertile@earthlink.net

DAVE KLUG

2304 James Street

McKeesport, PA 15132

412.754.KLUG Fax: 412.754.9881

601.991.0303
phone & fax
Email: cgaley@netdoor.com
For more samples, please view my website: www2.netdoor.com/~cgaley

SHEILA BAILEY

CHRISTINE BENJAMIN

DOMINIC CATALANO

SIRI WEBER FEENEY

CARLOS FREIRE

JOSEPH HAMMOND

SUSAN JAEKEL

RENATE LOHMANN

PEG MAGOVERN

DOUG ROY

WENDY RUDICK SHAUL

DJ SIMISON

MARTHA WESTON

REPRESENTED
BY
ANN REMEN-WILLIS

CEO TREATS

SHEILA BAILEY

RENATE LOHMANN

REPRESENTED BY
2964 COLTON RD, PEBBLE BEACH, CA 93953

ANN REMEN-WILLIS
831 ▪ 655 ▪ 1407 TEL, 831 ▪ 655 ▪ 1408 FAX

DOMINIC CATALANO

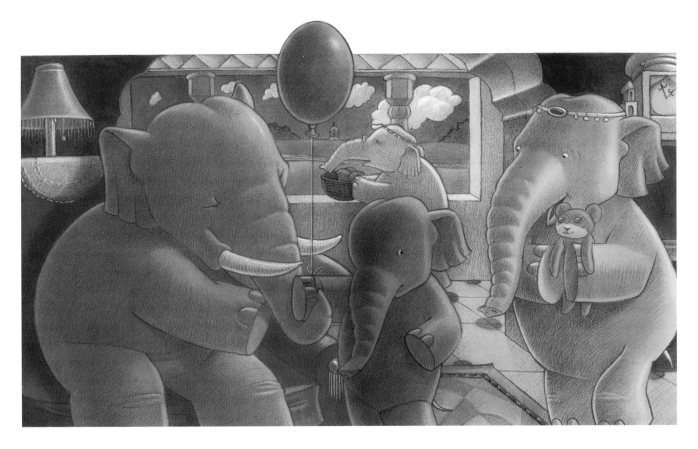

REPRESENTED BY ANN REMEN-WILLIS
2964 COLTON RD, PEBBLE BEACH, CA 93953 831 · 655 · 1407 TEL, 831 · 655 · 1408 FAX

SUSAN JAEKEL

REPRESENTED BY   ANN REMEN-WILLIS
2964 COLTON RD, PEBBLE BEACH, CA 93953   831 ▪ 655 ▪ 1407 TEL, 831 ▪ 655 ▪ 1408 FAX

DJ Simison

REPRESENTED BY **ANN REMEN-WILLIS**
2964 COLTON RD, PEBBLE BEACH, CA 93953   831▪655▪1407 TEL, 831▪655▪1408 FAX

DOUG ROY

CARLOS FREIRE

PEG MAGOVERN

REPRESENTED BY
2964 COLTON RD, PEBBLE BEACH, CA 93953

ANN REMEN-WILLIS
831 · 655 · 1407 TEL, 831 · 655 · 1408 FAX

MARTHA WESTON

JOSEPH HAMMOND

REPRESENTED BY

2964 COLTON RD, PEBBLE BEACH, CA 93953

ANN REMEN-WILLIS

831 • 655 • 1407 TEL, 831 • 655 • 1408 FAX

WENDY RUDICK SHAUL

REPRESENTED BY ANN REMEN-WILLIS
2964 COLTON RD, PEBBLE BEACH, CA 93953   831·655·1407 TEL, 831·655·1408 FAX

SIRI WEBER FEENEY

REPRESENTED BY   ANN REMEN-WILLIS
2964 COLTON RD, PEBBLE BEACH, CA 93953   831 ▪ 655 ▪ 1407 TEL, 831 ▪ 655 ▪ 1408 FAX

CHRISTINE BENJAMIN

REPRESENTED BY ANN REMEN-WILLIS

2964 COLTON RD, PEBBLE BEACH, CA 93953   831 ▪ 655 ▪ 1407 TEL, 831 ▪ 655 ▪ 1408 FAX

CHRISTINE BENJAMIN

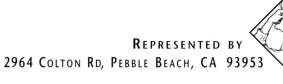

REPRESENTED BY   ANN REMEN-WILLIS
2964 COLTON RD, PEBBLE BEACH, CA 93953   831 ∙ 655 ∙ 1407 TEL, 831 ∙ 655 ∙ 1408 FAX

cyd moore • 248·723·0847 • fax: 248·723·0914

 see more art: www.cydmoore.com
and on www.picture-book.com

Jennifer Emery

2405 3rd Avenue South A14 • Minneapolis, MN 55404

612.872.1026 cell: 612.616.4864

Karen Bell

310.457.3943

Chad Cameron
WWW.CHADCAMERON.COM

DAWN W. MAJEWSKI

3116 Addison Court
Bensalem, PA 19020
215.752.4879/Fax 215.752.4879

From *On the Day His Daddy Left* • by Eric J. Adams & Kathleen Adams, L.C.S.W. • Illustrations © 2000 by Layne Johnson • Published by Albert Whitman & Co.

Layne Johnson

281 • 469 • 1133

laynejohnson.com laynejo@swbell.net Member Society of Children's Book Writers and Illustrators

mARTin lemelMAN
1-888-412-1960
1-610-395-4536

Cecilia Noyes

California Studio

562-799-8866

472 Schooner Way
Seal Beach, CA 90740

cdnoyes@home.com

Baga Yaga   Russian Folktale

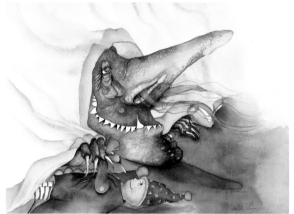

Gryla   Icelandic Folktale

Tide Pool

Road Hog

Don Daily

610.664.5729 • FAX: 610.664.7560

BETH BUFFINGTON

Sheryl Beranbaum Artists' Representative • Tel 401 737 8591 • Fax 401 739 5189 • www.beranbaum.com

BROCK NICOL

Sheryl Beranbaum Artists' Representative • Tel 401 737 8591 • Fax 401 739 5189 • www.beranbaum.com

Karen Silverman
153 Avenue B Apt. 5
New York, N.Y. 10009
(212) 477-3439

rangner

Mike Rangner 1647 N.E. 142nd Portland, Or. 97230 P (503) 262-7313 F (503) 262-7314

Susan Gross

illustrations & monotypes
415.751.5879
www.susangross.com

GIRLS GO GLOBAL

MY Life as a Leaf.

Kitties, kittens

dogs gone wrong!

BOOKMAKERS LTD.

We don't just make books. We create success stories.

For 25 years Bookmakers has represented a group of the best children's book illustrators in the business and provided the publishing industry with book design and production services.

We've worked with most major publishers and look forward to helping create a success story out of *your* next project.

P.O. Box 1086, 40 Mouse House Road, Taos, NM 87571 • (505)776-5435 • Fax(505)776-2762
email: bookmakers@newmex.com • website: bookmakersltd.com

BOOKMAKERS LTD

BOOKMAKERS LTD.

Representing
KATHI McCORD

"I have a song to sing. "Art is my voice and the characters I create are my sometimes harmonious, sometimes cacophonous chorus."
———*Kathi*

P.O. Box 1086, 40 Mouse House Road, Taos, NM 87571 • (505)776-5435 • Fax(505)776-2762
email: bookmakers@newmex.com • website: bookmakersltd.com

BOOKMAKERS LTD.

Representing
SUSAN BANTA

"The characters that I draw provide me with company while I work.
"They're pets, friends and, ultimately, my children."
——*Susan*

P.O. Box 1086, 40 Mouse House Road, Taos, NM 87571 • (505)776-5435 • Fax(505)776-2762
email: bookmakers@newmex.com • website: bookmakersltd.com

BOOKMAKERS LTD.

"Illustration is for me, a childhood dream come true. It is to do what I have done since I was three: imagine and read stories and make them real on paper.

"My goal is to show the viewer a glimpse of their own youth and draw them back to a time too long forgotten."

———*Amy*

BOOKMAKERS LTD

Representing
TED MCNEIL

"Doing illustrations for children
allows me to become more childlike for awhile.
"My world becomes less complicated and
time stands still.

"Nature, creatures and children exist together
as a happy, idyllic whole. Kindness abounds.
"It's a good life."
———Ted

P.O. Box 1086, 40 Mouse House Road, Taos, NM 87571 • (505)776-5435 • Fax(505)776-2762
email: bookmakers@newmex.com • website: bookmakersltd.com

BOOKMAKERS LTD.

Representing
JUDITH MITCHELL

"Illustrating for children is like a magical theater: characters become real for me and their expressions, gestures, costumes and settings all come alive. "I love it!"
————*Judith*

P.O. Box 1086, 40 Mouse House Road, Taos, NM 87571 • (505)776-5435 • Fax(505)776-2762
email: bookmakers@newmex.com • website: bookmakersltd.com

BOOKMAKERS LTD

Representing
ROBIN BRICKMAN
Cut and painted paper sculpture

"From a conventional sketch, an illustration is created by cutting, painting hand-sculpting and gluing paper.

"For me, the process itself is magical and fun...like dancing without gravity."
——Robin

P.O. Box 1086, 40 Mouse House Road, Taos, NM 87571 • (505)776-5435 • Fax(505)776-2762
email: bookmakers@newmex.com • website: bookmakersltd.com

BOOKMAKERS LTD.

Representing
DAVID BROOKS

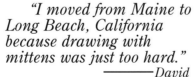

"I moved from Maine to Long Beach, California because drawing with mittens was just too hard."
———David

P.O. Box 1086, 40 Mouse House Road, Taos, NM 87571 • (505)776-5435 • Fax(505)776-2762
email: bookmakers@newmex.com • website: bookmakersltd.com

BOOKMAKERS LTD

Representing
MARSHA SERAFIN
Cut-paper illustration

"I'm always attracted by the combination of bright colors with mixed patterns in my illustrations...a sort of cut-paper crazy quilt."
——*Marsha*

Hey Diddle Diddle the Cat and the Fiddle

The cow jumped over the moon.

The little dog laughed to see such fun...

and the dish ran away with the spoon

P.O. Box 1086, 40 Mouse House Road, Taos, NM 87571 • (505)776-5435 • Fax(505)776-2762
email: bookmakers@newmex.com • website: bookmakersltd.com

BOOKMAKERS LTD.

Representing
MARSHA SERAFIN
Cut-paper illustration

P.O. Box 1086, 40 Mouse House Road, Taos, NM 87571 • (505)776-5435 • Fax(505)776-2762
email: bookmakers@newmex.com • website: bookmakersltd.com

BOOKMAKERS LTD

BOOKMAKERS LTD.

Representing
DAVID HOHN

"There is no greater satisfaction than to kindle a child's imagination. That is my challenge each time I put brush to paper."
——David

P.O. Box 1086, 40 Mouse House Road, Taos, NM 87571 • (505)776-5435 • Fax(505)776-2762
email: bookmakers@newmex.com • website: bookmakersltd.com

BOOKMAKERS LTD

Representing
KAREN PELLATON

"Life is full of ambiguities...except when I'm putting pen to paper."
———*Karen*

P.O. Box 1086, 40 Mouse House Road, Taos, NM 87571 • (505)776-5435 • Fax(505)776-2762
email: bookmakers@newmex.com • website: bookmakersltd.com

BOOKMAKERS LTD.

Representing
DICK SMOLINSKI

"Every word, every picture counts...kids are an astute audience."
——*Dick*

P.O. Box 1086, 40 Mouse House Road, Taos, NM 87571 • (505)776-5435 • Fax(505)776-2762
email: bookmakers@newmex.com • website: bookmakersltd.com

• Cheryl Nobens • Phone & Fax: 952-935-9130 • canobens@uscorp.net • 3616 Rhode Island Ave. So., St. Louis Park MN 55426

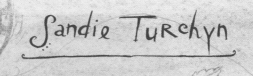

Sandie Turchyn

tel 310.275.8877
web-site: www.sandieturchyn.com
e-mail: sturchyn@aol.com

310.
275
8877

SANDIE TURCHYN

Mary York
illustration

3015 magnolia place • hattiesburg, mississippi 39401 • (601) 271-2954 • marypyork@earthlink.net

Kris Wiltse
morgangaynin.com

Fiona King

Box 232722 • Encinitas, CA 92023

760.942.1121 • 888.522.3745

Jackie Urbanovic

Terrific Teasers

What kind of tree barks?
A dogwood.

Why did the musician spend so much time in bed?
Because she was writing sheet music.

What did one flea say to the other?
"Shall we walk home or take the greyhound?"

How do you spot a leopard in the jungle?
You can't, it's already spotted.

What has brown and black fur and a million sharp teeth?

I don't know either, but there's one on your shoulder!

I don't know. What?

Art by Jaci Urbanovic

25

Jackie Urbanovic
301.495.9481 • fax 301.587.6322

Harcourt Brace

RAMUNE 781-444-1185 NEEDHAM, MA 02494

Heather Knopf

12 Wendell Street #17

Cambridge, MA 02138

617.491.6407

heather@hmkcreative.com

www.hmkcreative.com

DREW ROSE
ILLUSTRATION

770-460-8438
WILL SUMPTER
&ASSOCIATES

MARY ROSS
Illustration

Jane Dippold

Laurie Lambert & Associates Inc.

TELEPHONE 513.774.8777
FACSIMILE 513.774.8603
www.lambertassociatesinc.com

Tammie Lyon

Laurie Lambert & Associates Inc.

TELEPHONE 513.774.8777
FACSIMILE 513.774.8603
www.lambertassociatesinc.com

Laurie Lambert & Associates Inc.

TELEPHONE 513.774.8777
FACSIMILE 513.774.8603
www.lambertassociatesinc.com

Laura Merer

Kathy Couri

Laurie Lambert & Associates Inc.

TELEPHONE 513.774.8777
FACSIMILE 513.774.8603
www.lambertassociatesinc.com

CHERYL NATHAN
ILLUSTRATION/DESIGN

9495 Evergreen Place #406/ Ft. Lauderdale, FL 33324 · 954/476-7819 · E-mail: cnathan@mail.idt.net

An **African elephant!**

Mom, look how cool!
Please watch it tomorrow
while I go to school.

Bernard Adnet

Craven Design Studios, Inc. 234 Fifth Avenue New York, New York 10001
Telephone 212 696.4680   Fax 212 532.2626   www.cravendesignstudios.com

CRAVENDESIGN **Craven Design Studios, Inc.** 234 Fifth Avenue New York, New York 10001
Telephone 212 696.4680 Fax 212 532.2626 www.cravendesignstudios.com

Craven Design Studios, Inc. 234 Fifth Avenue New York, New York 10001
Telephone 212 696.4680   Fax 212 532.2626   www.cravendesignstudios.com

CRAVENDESIGN   **Craven Design Studios, Inc.** 234 Fifth Avenue New York, New York 10001
Telephone 212 696.4680   Fax 212 532.2626   www.cravendesignstudios.com

Craven Design Studios, Inc. 234 Fifth Avenue New York, New York 10001
Telephone 212 696.4680 Fax 212 532.2626 www.cravendesignstudios.com

CRAVENDESIGN

Gershom Griffith

Craven Design Studios, Inc. 234 Fifth Avenue New York, New York 10001
Telephone 212 696.4680 Fax 212 532.2626 www.cravendesignstudios.com

Diana Magnuson

STORY VINE™

Eagle Feathers

Owl Goingback
Illustrated by Diana Magnuson

ISBN: 0-7802-8323-6

CRAVENDESIGN **Craven Design Studios, Inc.** 234 Fifth Avenue New York, New York 10001
Telephone 212 696.4680 Fax 212 532.2626 www.cravendesignstudios.com

Craven Design Studios, Inc. 234 Fifth Avenue New York, New York 10001
Telephone 212 696.4680 Fax 212 532.2626 www.cravendesignstudios.com

Charles Shaw

Craven Design Studios, Inc. 234 Fifth Avenue New York, New York 10001
Telephone 212 696.4680 Fax 212 532.2626 www.cravendesignstudios.com **CRAVEN**DESIGN

Pamela Carroll

Mordicai Gerstein

CRAVENDESIGN   **Craven Design Studios, Inc.** 234 Fifth Avenue New York, New York 10001
Telephone 212 696.4680   Fax 212 532.2626   www.cravendesignstudios.com

Vickie Learner

N. Jo Tufts

Craven Design Studios, Inc. 234 Fifth Avenue New York, New York 10001
Telephone 212 696.4680   Fax 212 532.2626   www.cravendesignstudios.com   **CRAVEN**DESIGN

Suzette Barbier

124 Winchester Street
Newton, MA 02461
email: artwork@suzettebarbier.com
website: suzettebarbier.com

We'll invite flying fish and give each one a dish full of cookies and treats from the sea.

Mm

Manny Moon

Manny Moon can mix a cake
And munch a macaroon.
Can Manny make a muffin
On a Monday afternoon?

18

Louise Max

phone: 802-297-2976 • fax: 802-297-0090

P.O. Box 272 • Jamaica, VT 05343

Kristin Rauchenstein

223 James Road • Gahanna, OH 43202
614.476.2134 • email: krauchenstein@hotmail.com

Visit Wendell Minor at minorart.com

KIM PASSEY

CHRIS LENSCH

LIZ SANDERS AGENCY
TELEPHONE: (949) 495-3664   FACSIMILE: (949) 495-0129   WWW.LIZSANDERS.COM

TOM PANSINI

AMY NING

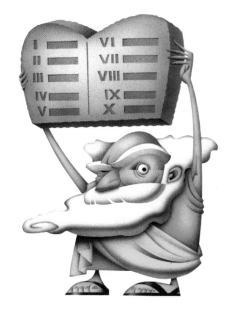

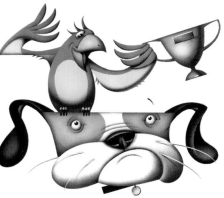

LIZ SANDERS AGENCY

TELEPHONE: (949) 495-3664   FACSIMILE: (949) 495-0129   WWW.LIZSANDERS.COM

Matthew Ambre Illustration

743 W. Brompton Ave.• Chicago, IL 60657
773.935.5170 • fax: 773.935.5748

Marlena
(agenCy]

T. 609 252-9405
F. 609 252-1949

www.marlenaagency.com

Marc Mongeau

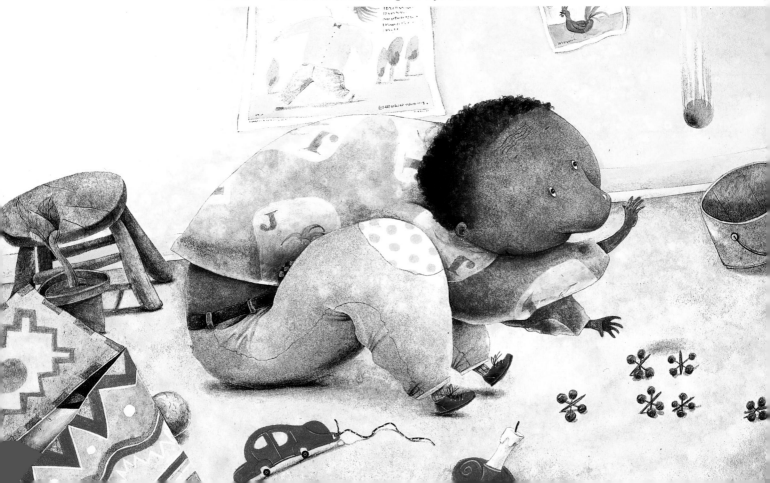

M

Marlena
(agenCy)

T. 609 252-9405
F. 609 252-1949

www.marlenaagency.com

Marlena (aGenCy)

T. 609 252-9405
F. 609 252-1949
www.marlenaagency.com

Normand Cousineau

margaret anne suggs
illustrator and designer

59 Stratford Haven
Orwell Road
Rathgar
Dublin 6, Ireland

+353 86 6073986
margaretanne@georgia.com
www.margaretannesuggs.com

phone/fax: 973•743•8691

JODY JOBE

e-mail: jodyjobe@mindspring.com

MEREDITH JOHNSON • 5228 PALM DRIVE • LA CAÑADA, CA 91011 • 818-790-8060 • FAX: 818-790-1709

meredithdraws@earthlink.net

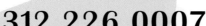

STUDIOS, LLC

Linda Howard Bittner

901 West Jackson Blvd. Suite 201 Chicago IL 60607   telephone 312.226.0007 facsimile 312.226.0404

Phyllis Pollema-Cahill

901 West Jackson Blvd. Suite 201 Chicago IL 60607   telephone 312.226.0007 facsimile 312.226.0404

Donna Catanese

Wilkinson
STUDIOS, LLC

901 West Jackson Blvd. Suite 201 Chicago IL 60607   telephone 312.226.0007 facsimile 312.226.0404

Mike Dammer

Wilkinson
STUDIOS, LLC

901 West Jackson Blvd. Suite 201 Chicago IL 60607   telephone 312.226.0007 facsimile 312.226.0404

Marion Eldridge

901 West Jackson Blvd. Suite 201 Chicago IL 60607   telephone 312.226.0007 facsimile 312.226.0404

Dan Grant

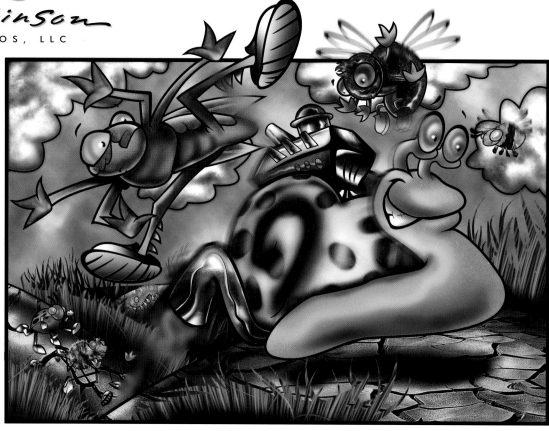

Toby Williams

901 West Jackson Blvd. Suite 201 Chicago IL 60607   telephone 312.226.0007 facsimile 312.226.0404

Patti Green

901 West Jackson Blvd. Suite 201 Chicago IL 60607   telephone 312.226.0007 facsimile 312.226.0404

Wilkinson
STUDIOS, LLC

Johanna Hantel

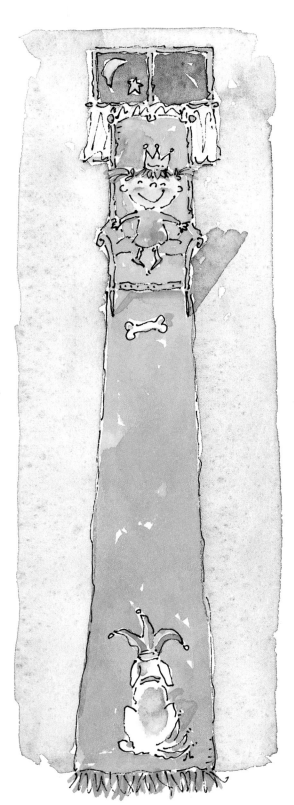

901 West Jackson Blvd. Suite 201 Chicago IL 60607   telephone 312.226.0007 facsimile 312.226.0404

April Hartmann

901 West Jackson Blvd. Suite 201 Chicago IL 60607   telephone 312.226.0007 facsimile 312.226.0404

CD Hullinger

901 West Jackson Blvd. Suite 201 Chicago IL 60607   telephone 312.226.0007 facsimile 312.226.0404

Freddie Levin

901 West Jackson Blvd. Suite 201 Chicago IL 60607   telephone 312.226.0007 facsimile 312.226.0404

Bob Masheris

Wilkinson
STUDIOS, LLC

901 West Jackson Blvd. Suite 201 Chicago IL 60607   telephone 312.226.0007 facsimile 312.226.0404

STUDIOS, LLC

Chris Pappas

901 West Jackson Blvd. Suite 201 Chicago IL 60607 telephone 312.226.0007 facsimile 312.226.0404

Wilkinson
STUDIOS, LLC

Guy Porfirio

901 West Jackson Blvd. Suite 201 Chicago IL 60607   telephone 312.226.0007 facsimile 312.226.0404

Wendy Rasmussen

901 West Jackson Blvd. Suite 201 Chicago IL 60607   telephone 312.226.0007 facsimile 312.226.0404

901 West Jackson Blvd. Suite 201 Chicago IL 60607   telephone 312.226.0007 facsimile 312.226.0404

Ilene Richard

COREY

360.
687.
0699

WOLFE

JOHN HANLEY
ILLUSTRATION

815 459 1123

134

Steve **ELLIS**

Please see Picturebook 2K , previous Black Book
and Directory of Illustration publications

Madeline **VASQUEZ**

P 503.658.7070
f 503.658.3960

christine prapas --- **represented by**

doug HORNE

Digital

represented by -- christine prapas

P 503.658.7070
f 503.658.3960
www.christineprapas.com

Angelina **MARINO**

Editorial

P 503.658.7070
f 503.658.3960
www.christineprapas.com

christine prapas --- **represented by**

Marla BAGGETTA

artist studio *marla baggetta*
phone 503.699.5049
fax 503.699.6457
marlaart.com

karyn SERVIN

p 503.658.7070
f 503.658.3960
www.christineprapas.com

christine prapas -- **represented by**

Kim MALEK

Bridgetown Printing

Fox Creative Group

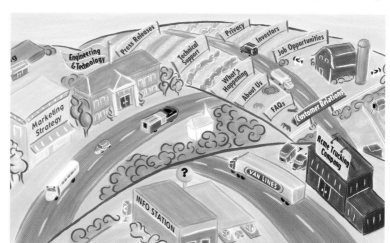

Freightliner Corporation

American Cancer Society

christine prapas

www.malekstudio.com
kmalek@malekstudio.com

p 503.658.7070
f 503.658.3960
www.christineprapas.com

represented by ---

Joanne Scribner.com

Cathy Morrison
Big Chief Graphics

720 493 1954
fax: 720 493 1948
e-mail: bigchief10@aol.com
www.cathymorrison.com
6209 South Grape Court
Littleton, Colorado 80121

GREG HARRIS

2-D Cross Highway, Westport, CT 06880
Ph:(203) 454-4210, Fax:(203) 454-4258, E Mail:CMartreps@aol.com
www.cornellandmccarthy.com

LAURA RADER

2-D Cross Highway, Westport, CT 06880
.Ph:(203) 454-4210, Fax:(203) 454-4258, E Mail:CMartreps@aol.com
www.cornellandmccarthy.com

DAVID T. WENZEL

2-D Cross Highway, Westport, CT 06880
.Ph:(203) 454-4210, Fax:(203) 454-4258, E Mail:CMartreps@aol.com
www.cornellandmccarthy.com

BENTON MAHAN

2-D Cross Highway, Westport, CT 06880
.Ph:(203) 454-4210, Fax:(203) 454-4258, E Mail:CMartreps@aol.com
www.cornellandmccarthy.com

RENÉE GRAEF

2-D Cross Highway, Westport, CT 06880
Ph:(203) 454-4210, Fax:(203) 454-4258, E Mail:CMartreps@aol.com
www.cornellandmccarthy.com

DORIS ETTLINGER

2-D Cross Highway, Westport, CT 06880
.Ph:(203) 454-4210, Fax:(203) 454-4258, E Mail:CMartreps@aol.com
www.cornellandmccarthy.com

150

Morning Song Henry Holt & Co. © 2001 Elizabeth Sayles

ELIZABETH SAYLES

2-D Cross Highway, Westport, CT 06880
.Ph:(203) 454-4210, Fax:(203) 454-4258, E Mail:CMartreps@aol.com
www.cornellandmccarthy.com

ROSE MARY BERLIN

2-D Cross Highway, Westport, CT 06880
.Ph:(203) 454-4210, Fax:(203) 454-4258, E Mail:CMartreps@aol.com
www.cornellandmccarthy.com

ANNI MATSICK

2-D Cross Highway, Westport, CT 06880
Ph:(203) 454-4210, Fax:(203) 454-4258, E Mail:CMartreps@aol.com
www.cornellandmccarthy.com

RUSTY FLETCHER

2-D Cross Highway, Westport, CT 06880
.Ph:(203) 454-4210, Fax:(203) 454-4258, E Mail:CMartreps@aol.com
www.cornellandmccarthy.com

RUSTY FLETCHER

2-D Cross Highway, Westport, CT 06880
.Ph:(203) 454-4210, Fax:(203) 454-4258, E Mail:CMartreps@aol.com
www.cornellandmccarthy.com

KATE FLANAGAN

ESTHER SZEGEDY

2-D Cross Highway, Westport, CT 06880
Ph:(203) 454-4210, Fax:(203) 454-4258, E Mail:CMartreps@aol.com
www.cornellandmccarthy.com

ARTIST REPRESENTATIVES

ANDREA TACHIERA

ELLEN JOY SASAKI

2-D Cross Highway, Westport, CT 06880
Ph:(203) 454-4210, Fax:(203) 454-4258, E Mail:CMartreps@aol.com
www.cornellandmccarthy.com

CHRISTINE POWERS

CHERYL MENDENHALL

2-D Cross Highway, Westport, CT 06880
.Ph:(203) 454-4210, Fax:(203) 454-4258, E Mail:CMartreps@aol.com
www.cornellandmccarthy.com

YVETTE BANEK

MEG AUBREY

2-D Cross Highway, Westport, CT 06880
.Ph:(203) 454-4210, Fax:(203) 454-4258, E Mail:CMartreps@aol.com
www.cornellandmccarthy.com

Eva M. Schlesinger

snoogle@earthlink.net
510.665.5788

selina alko

718.768.8133
www.theispot.com/artist/alko

alcolors@aol.com

BEATRIZ VIDAL

REPRESENTED (by) **WANDA NOWAK** PHONE 212·535·0438   FAX 212·535·1624

www.wandanow.com

ANDI BUTLER

720 Bay Berry Drive • Cary, IL 60013
phone: 847.462.9091 • fax: 847.462.9094
e-mail: nutlab@mc.net

Bob Berry Illustration & Design, Inc.
38 Deerview Lane, Poughquag, NY 12570
845-223-7925- phone and fax
e-mail: cyansevant@aol.com, cyan@bestweb.net

Digital and Traditional Illustration for:
- Picture books
- Editorial
- Religious
- Activity books
- Text Books
- Advertising

Dragon Tales- © 2000 Children's Television Workshop / Random House Children's Books

© 2000 Harcourt School Publishers

© 2000 Harcourt School Publishers

© 2000 Harcourt School Publishers

© 2000 Fisher Price and Reader's Digest Children's Publishing

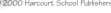

JACKIE SNIDER
(705) 924-1487

lynn JEFFERY

harry MOORE

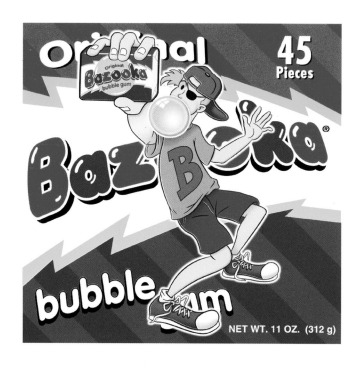

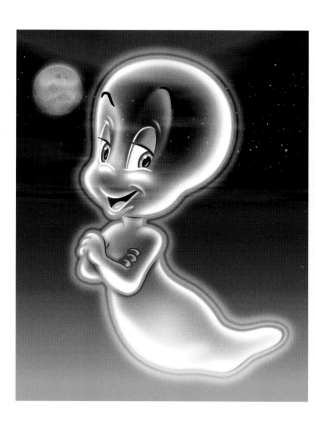

nancy HARRISON

leif PENG

215.232.6666   fax 215.232.6585   www.deborahwolfeltd.com   **DEBORAH WOLFE LTD**
731 N 24th St., Philadelphia, PA 19130

dave GARBOT

cindy REVELL

215.232.6666   fax 215.232.6585   www.deborahwolfeltd.com   **DEBORAH WOLFE LTD**
731 N 24th St., Philadelphia, PA 19130

170

amy WUMMER

debra SPINA DIXON

215.232.6666   fax 215.232.6585   www.deborahwolfeltd.com   **DEBORAH WOLFE LTD**
731 N 24th St., Philadelphia, PA 19130

Deborah Perez-Stable

4080 Diane Drive
Fairview Park, Ohio 44126

440.331.5172
onelightsource@aol.com

Judge Cohen

9402 Belfort Road • Richmond, VA 23229
Ph/Fax 804.741.5061 • judcohen@erols.com
www.reuben.org/jcohen

Square Moon

6 Monterey Terrace
Orinda, CA 94563
925-253-9451
fax 925-253-9452
email: info@sqmoon.com

For more than twenty years, Square Moon artists have been creating illustrations to enhance children's books, textbooks, and educational materials.

Whether our clients publish in print or on the web, Square Moon artists have the experience, skill, and talent necessary to create the very best in communication design.

To see more samples of each artist's work, visit our website at **www.sqmoon.com**.

Visit our website at: **www.sqmoon.com**

Take a look at the out-of-this-wor

Cindy Brodie

Doug Roy

Gay Holland

Roseanne Litzinger

A Wise Owl
Lived in an Oak

Nancy Tobin

Nancy Woodman

Joseph Hammond

Jennifer DeCristoforo

Cindy Salans Rosenheim

Stan Tusan

Mas Miyamoto

Winson Trang

Jill Dubin

2070 Abby Lane• Atlanta, GA 30345 • phone 404.634.1650 • fax 404.634.0096

ERICA MAGNUS

15 Ondis Avenue   Athens, Ohio 45701
Fax/Phone: (740) 593-7883   emagnus@froget.net

PORTFOLIO

representing

Tiphanie Beeke	Renée Daily	Kristin Kest	Valeria Petrone
Robin Bell Corfield	Jack E. Davis	Albert Lemant	Mike Reed
John Bendall-Brunello	Eldon Doty	Anthony Lewis	Mick Reid
Nan Brooks	Kathi Ember	Stephen Lewis	Clive Scruton
Lindy Burnett	Mike Gordon	Katherine Lodge	Rémy Simard
Carlos Caban	Leonid Gore	Margeaux Lucas	Jamie Smith
Anthony Carnabuci	Amanda Harvey	John Manders	Theresa Smith
Abby Carter	Shelly Hehenberger	Paul Meisel	Kristina Stephenson
Randy Chewning	Laura Huliska-Beith	Julie Monks	Peggy Tagel
David Austin Clar	Judy Jarrett	Hiroe Nakata	Thomas Taylor
Steve Cox	Susan Keeter	Colin Paine	George Ulrich
Carolyn Croll	Anne Kennedy	Jan Palmer	John Wallace

visit us on the internet at

http://www.hkportfolio.com

Tiphanie Beeke

Robin Bell Corfield

John Bendall-Brunello

Nan Brooks

Harriet Kasak

TELEPHONE 212•675•5719
FACSIMILE 212•675•6341
E•MAIL harriet@hkportfolio.com
www.hkportfolio.com

Lindy Burnett

Carlos Caban

Anthony Carnabuci

Abby Carter

Harriet Kasak

TELEPHONE 212•675•5719
FACSIMILE 212•675•6341
E•MAIL harriet@hkportfolio.com
www.hkportfolio.com

Randy Chewning

David Austin Clar

Steve Cox

Carolyn Croll

Harriet Kasak

TELEPHONE 212•675•5719
FACSIMILE 212•675•6341
E•MAIL harriet@hkportfolio.com
www.hkportfolio.com

182

Renée Daily

Kathi Ember

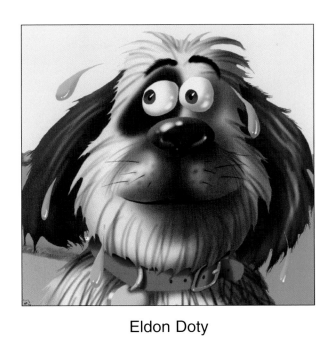

Eldon Doty

Jack E. Davis

Harriet Kasak

TELEPHONE 212•675•5719
FACSIMILE 212•675•6341
E•MAIL harriet@hkportfolio.com
www.hkportfolio.com

183

Mike Gordon

Leonid Gore

Amanda Harvey

Shelly Hehenberger

Harriet Kasak

TELEPHONE 212•675•5719
FACSIMILE 212•675•6341
E•MAIL harriet@hkportfolio.com
www.hkportfolio.com

Laura Huliska-Beith

Judy Jarrett

Susan Keeter

Anne Kennedy

Harriet Kasak

TELEPHONE 212•675•5719
FACSIMILE 212•675•6341
E•MAIL harriet@hkportfolio.com
www.hkportfolio.com

Kristin Kest

Albert Lemant

Anthony Lewis

Stephen Lewis

Harriet Kasak

TELEPHONE 212•675•5719
FACSIMILE 212•675•6341
E•MAIL harriet@hkportfolio.com
www.hkportfolio.com

186

Katherine Lodge

Margeaux Lucas

John Manders

Paul Meisel

Harriet Kasak

TELEPHONE 212•675•5719
FACSIMILE 212•675•6341
E•MAIL harriet@hkportfolio.com
www.hkportfolio.com

Julie Monks

Hiroe Nakata

Colin Paine

Jan Palmer

Harriet Kasak

TELEPHONE 212•675•5719
FACSIMILE 212•675•6341
E•MAIL harriet@hkportfolio.com
www.hkportfolio.com

Valeria Petrone

Michael Reed

Mick Reid

Clive Scruton

Harriet Kasak

TELEPHONE 212•675•5719
FACSIMILE 212•675•6341
E•MAIL harriet@hkportfolio.com
www.hkportfolio.com

Rémy Simard

Jamie Smith

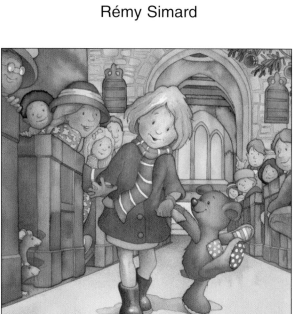

Kristina Stephenson

Peggy Tagel

Harriet Kasak

TELEPHONE 212•675•5719
FACSIMILE 212•675•6341
E•MAIL harriet@hkportfolio.com
www.hkportfolio.com

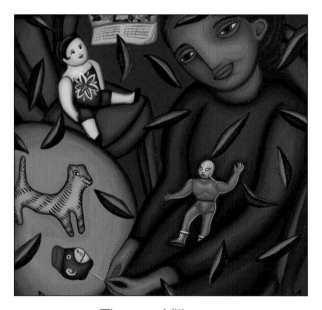

Thomas Taylor

George Ulrich

Theresa Villegas

John Wallace

Harriet Kasak

TELEPHONE 212•675•5719
FACSIMILE 212•675•6341
E•MAIL harriet@hkportfolio.com
www.hkportfolio.com

mikecressy@earthlink.net

MIKE CRESSY

ILLUSTRATION

4 2 5 0 6 0 3 0 9 6 6 9

On-line Portfolio

http://home.earthlink.net/~mikecressy

Susan Kathleen Hartung

517.592.5402 tel/fax
Brooklyn, MI 49230
www.susanhartung.com

karen williams

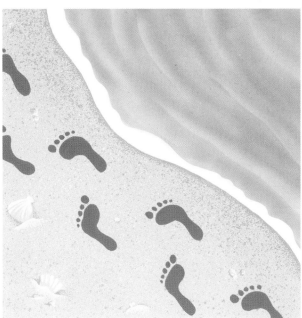

765 Milton Turnpike Highland, New York 12528
tel. 845-883-9007 email. VWGoe@aol.com

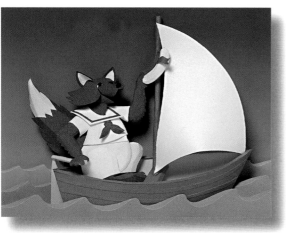

Eileen Mueller Neill
1500 Shawnee Trail
Riverwoods, Illinois 60015
Phone/Fax 847 948 0506
EileensPortfolio@aol.com
www.EileensPortfolio.com

196

red hansen

amy bates

steve brodner

james bernardin

lynne cannoy

jim carroll

sally wern compo

mark elliott

patrick faricy

guy francis

new york 212.333.2551
los angeles 323.874.5700
washington dc 410.349.8669
london 011.44.207.636.1064

dave gordon

brett helquist

michael koelsch

jim madsen

cliff nielsen

diane packer

greg swearingen

mike dietz

hala wittwer

Shannon

www.shannonassociates.com

Elizabeth Buttler
489 Old Stockbridge Road • Great Barrington, MA 01230
413.528.0604 fax: 413.528.0604

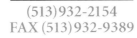

joe boddy•illustrator•406-251-3587

JEFF CLINE
HUMOROUS ILLUSTRATION

PHONE/FAX: (800)770-4089   EMAIL: jcillos@aol.com
www.jeffcline.com
50 Springholm Drive • Berkeley Heights, NJ 07922

ALAN FLINN

2720 East Yampa, Suite 221
Colorado Springs, CO 80909
719.389.0182

Kate Hosford

231 Berkeley Place, Apt. #2 • Brooklyn, NY 11217
718.398.3397 • khosford@hotmail.com

Dennis Higgins
122 Fifteenth Street, P.O. Box 385
Del Mar, California 92014
(858) 481-5017 Fax (858) 481-6270

Gwen Robinson

818.379.9978

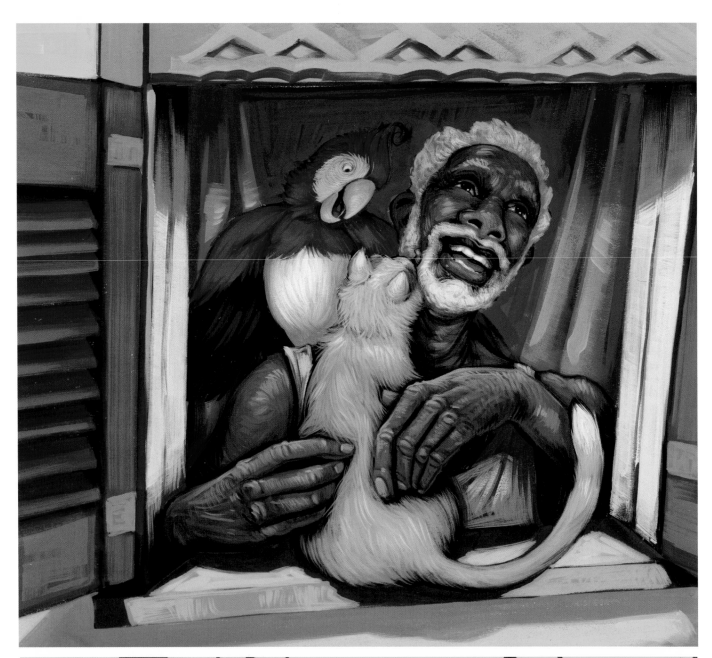

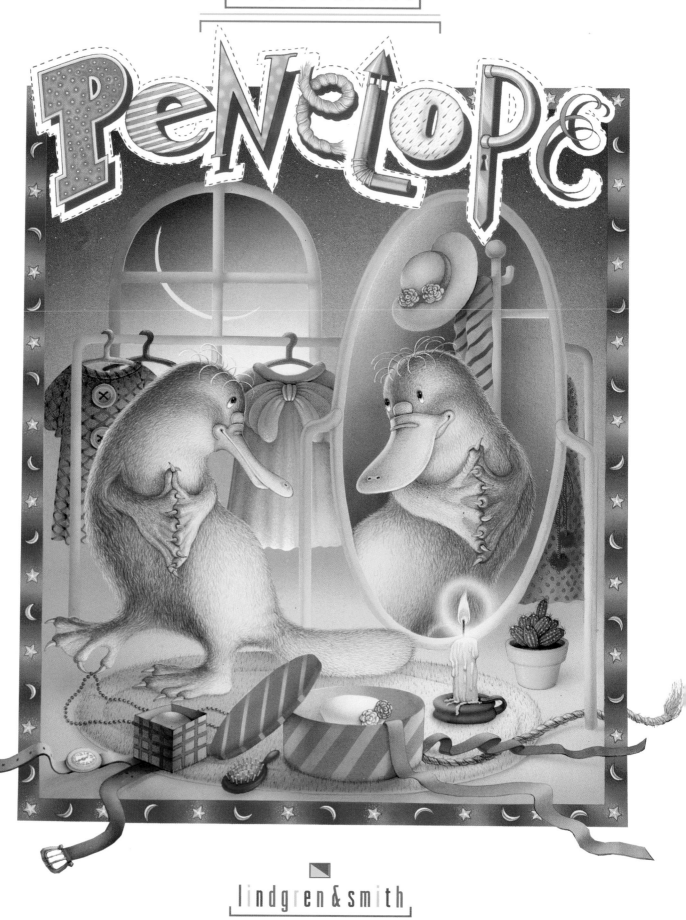

valerie sokolova

PENELOPE

lindgren&smith

new york 212.397.7330 >>> view portfolio at lindgrensmith.com >>> san francisco 415.788.85

lindgren&smith

steven salerno

lindgren&smith

w york 212.397.7330 >>> view portfolio at lindgrensmith.com >>> san francisco 415.788.8552

lindgren&smith

lindgren&smith

Karen Rhine
8027 Kilpatrick Ave.
Skokie, IL 60076
phone: 847-329-0837

e-mail: rhineline@anet.com
fax: 208-730-3223
website: www.anet-chi.com/~rhine/

member: Children's Book Insider
Society of Children's Book
Writers and Illustrators

KAREN C. RHINE ILLUSTRATION

Karen Rhine
8027 Kilpatrick Ave.
Skokie, IL 60076
phone: 847-329-0837

e-mail: rhineline@anet.com
fax: 208-730-3223
website: www.anet-chi.com/~rhine/

member: Children's Book Insider
Society of Children's Book
Writers and Illustrators

CHARLES STUBBS   **707.544.8358**

online portfolio: www.charlesstubbs.com   email: charles@charlesstubbs.com

638 Cordelia Drive #1, Santa Rosa, CA 95405

Fran
Lee

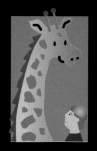

503.286.4767   www.coatimundistudios.com

KEN ROBERTS
772 Malcolm's Point Rd. • Cadiz, KY 42211
270.924.0078 • Fax: 270.924.0074

GRACE LIN

PO Box 401036
North Cambridge, MA 02140
1-888-798-6882 (tel/fax)
gracelin@concentric.net
www.gracelin.com

Zonderkidz Publishing "See the Country See the City" © 2000

Zonderkidz Publishing "See the Country See the City" © 2000

PAM THOMSON
ILLUSTRATION

GARRY COLBY
ILLUSTRATION

THE NEIS GROUP
ILLUSTRATION • DESIGN • PHOTOGRAPHY

11440 OAK DRIVE • P.O. BOX 174 • SHELBYVILLE, MICHIGAN 49344
TELEPHONE 616-672-5756 • FAX 616-672-5757 • www.neisgroup.com

DAN SHARP
ILLUSTRATION

TERRY WORKMAN
ILLUSTRATION

THE NEIS GROUP
ILLUSTRATION • DESIGN • PHOTOGRAPHY

11440 OAK DRIVE • P.O. BOX 174 • SHELBYVILLE, MICHIGAN 49344
TELEPHONE 616-672-5756 • FAX 616-672-5757 • www.neisgroup.com

Houghton Mifflin "The Carrot Countdown" © 2000

National Safe Kids Campaign / General Motors © 1999

ERIKA LɛBARRE
ILLUSTRATION

CLINT HANSEN
ILLUSTRATION

THE NEIS GROUP
ILLUSTRATION • DESIGN • PHOTOGRAPHY

11440 OAK DRIVE • P.O. BOX 174 • SHELBYVILLE, MICHIGAN 49344
TELEPHONE 616-672-5756 • FAX 616-672-5757 • www.neisgroup.com

228

Zonderkidz Publishing "Mornin' Mr. Ted!" © 2001

LIZ CONRAD
ILLUSTRATION

Zonderkidz Publishing "Zachary's Zoo" © 2000

LYN BOYER
ILLUSTRATION

THE NEIS GROUP
ILLUSTRATION • DESIGN • PHOTOGRAPHY

11440 OAK DRIVE • P.O. BOX 174 • SHELBYVILLE, MICHIGAN 49344
TELEPHONE 616-672-5756 • FAX 616-672-5757 • www.neisgroup.com

MIKE STEPANEK

847·670·9479

PAMELA R. LEVY

Ph./Fax (617) 254-5779 ◆ 7 Trapelo St. ◆ Brighton, MA ◆ 02135 ◆ pamelalevy@hotmail.com

Grove Illustration & Design in Vermont

802.273.2069
groveart@sover.net

Bob McMahon
bobmcmahon.com
818 955 8802

bobtoons@earthlink.net

233

Laurie Surah

6847 S. La Posada Place • Hereford, AZ 85615
p 520.378.3183 • f 520.459.7829
lsurah@hotmail.com

Susan Havice

6 Roundy Road

Lynnfield, MA 01940

phone/fax 781-334-3976

Janette Bach

Toll-Free: 877-749-3367
Fax: 425-586-6734

info@bachpro.com

12819 SE 38th St. #344
Bellevue, WA 98006-1395

www.bachpro.com

PEGGY DRESSEL

11 Rockaway Ave.
Oakland, NJ 07436

pegdartist@aol.com

phone/fax
201-337-2143

G A R Y   T O R R I S I

Tel (781) 235-8658 • Fax (781) 235-8635 • www.gwenwaltersartrep.com • e-mail ArtIncGW@aol.com

TOM BARRETT

DEBORAH WHITE

ARTISTS' REPRESENTATIVE

· GWEN WALTERS ·

JUDITH PFEIFFER

el (781) 235-8658 • Fax (781) 235-8635 • www.gwenwaltersartrep.com • e-mail ArtIncGW@aol.com

SALLY SCHAEDLER

PAT PARIS

el (781) 235-8658 • Fax (781) 235-8635 • www.gwenwaltersartrep.com • e-mail ArtIncGW@aol.com

ROSARIO VALDERRAMA

FABRICIO VANDENBROEK

GERARDO SUSAN

Tel (781) 235-8658 • Fax (781) 235-8635 • www.gwenwaltersartrep.com • e-mail ArtIncGW@aol.com

ARTISTS' REPRESENTATIVE

· GWEN WALTERS ·

JANICE SKIVINGTON

Tel (781) 235-8658 • Fax (781) 235-8635 • www.gwenwaltersartrep.com • e-mail ArtIncGW@aol.com

PHYLLIS HARRIS
illustration

phone & fax 816•331•6168

www.phyllisharris.com

phyllis@phyllisharris.com

"N" is for New York - Cover art
publication December 2000 - GHB Publishers

MARISOL SARRAZIN

marisol.sarrazin@sympatico.ca • Tel.: (450) 228-2255 • Fax: (450) 228-2855
1507 des Bécassines, Sainte-Adèle (Québec) CANADA J8B 2C3

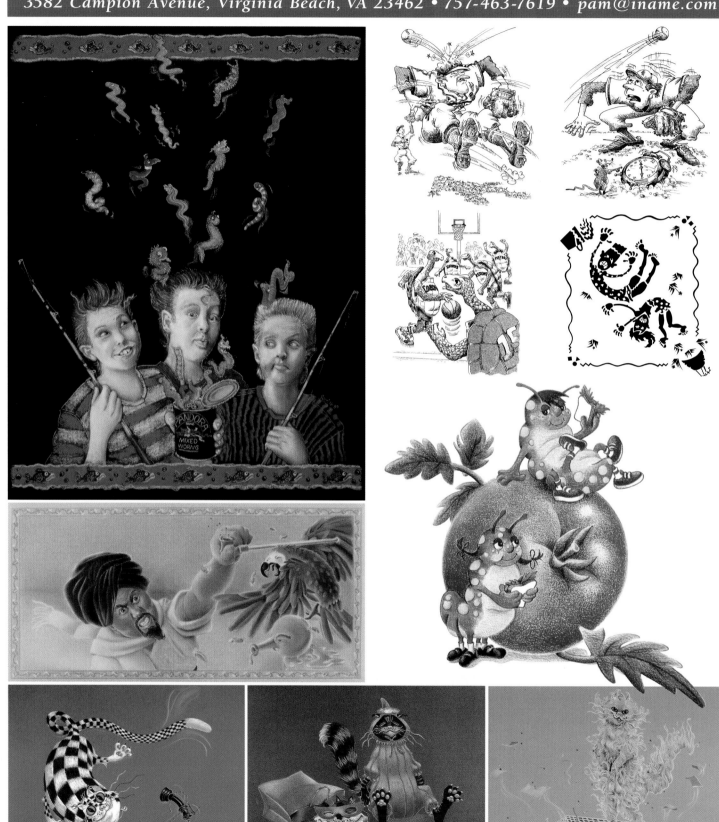

papier
cutz
STUDIO

Monika Popowitz
914-342-6945
email: papiercutz@citlink.net

www.happypix.com

Dear Diary,
Today I feel really
blue. My best friend is
mad at me and the
who sits behind me in
is

barbara POLLAK
digital illustration
(415) 550-0551

Liz Amini-Holmes

e-mail liz@lunavilla.com * web www.lunavilla.com * tel 650-851-3988

Karen Patkau

416 260 1915

401 Queens Quay West Suite 609 Toronto, Ontario

Canada, M5V 2Y2 Fax. 416 260 1916

254

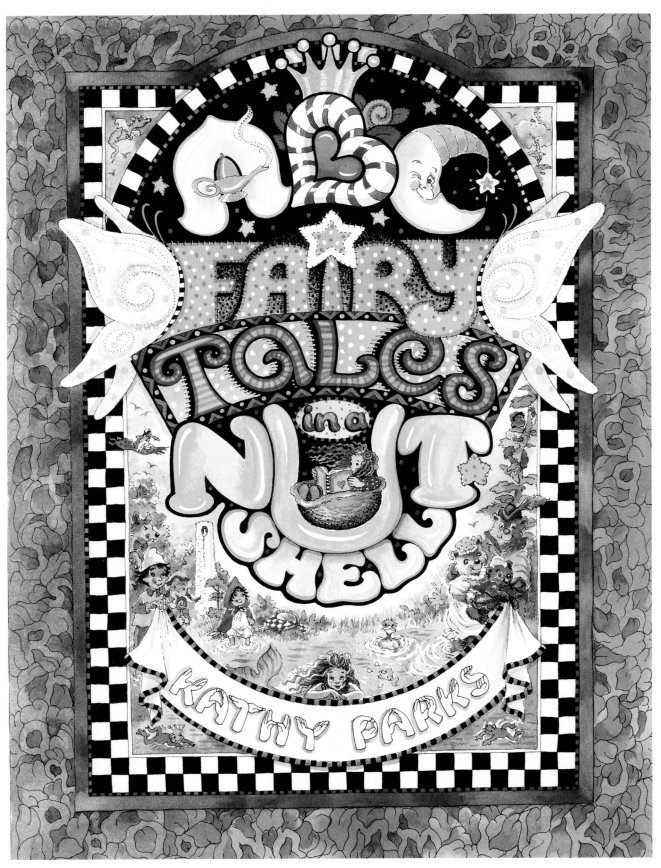

Kathy Parks

705 "E" Avenue • Coronado, CA 92118
phone/fax 619.435.0066

MARK PAGE

1520 West 8th Street #98

Upland, CA 91786

909.920.4227 Fax: 909.982.2451

e-mail: mpageca@earthlink.net

Larry Reinhart illustration

freakypaint@earthlink.net

909 790 5753

Jim Nuttle

I L L U S T R A T I O N

Phone: 301-989-0942
Fax: 301-989-1342
www.jimnuttle.com

Carol Bancroft & Friends represents
many artists who specialize in
illustrating children's materials,
including but not limited to
picture books.

On the next few pages
you will find a sampling of only a
few of the many artists we represent.
To view the entire collection of our
artists' work, we invite you
to visit our website.

www.carolbancroft.com

(800) 720-7020
artists@carolbancroft.com

© HIGGINS BOND

HIGGINS BOND

© PETER CHURCH/GARGOYLES "MONSTERS IN STONE"/GROSSET & DUNLAP

PETER CHURCH

© LOEK KOOPMANS/CINDERELLA/NORTH SOUTH BOOKS

LOEK KOOPMANS

REPRESENTED BY  (800) 720-7020

260

SUSAN GABER

REPRESENTED BY   CAROL BANCROFT & FRIENDS   (800) 720-7020

YOSHI MIYAKE

LORETTA LUSTIG

CARY PHILLIPS

DEBRAH SANTINI

REPRESENTED BY  (800) 720-7020

MARK OLSON

SCOTT MATTERN

SCOTT MATTERN

JENNIFER FITCHWELL

BLANCHE SIMS

BARRY ROCKWELL

REPRESENTED BY  (800) 720-7020

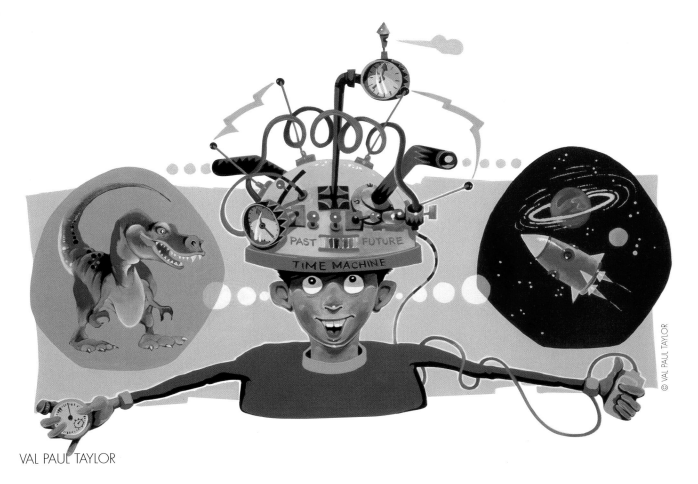

VAL PAUL TAYLOR

VAL PAUL TAYLOR

REPRESENTED BY **CAROL BANCROFT & FRIENDS** (800) 720-7020

DEAR MRS. MARSH

written by
ANDREW WILLETT

illustrated by
RICK STROMOSKI

Rick StroMoski

Represented by
The Penny & Stermer Group

Call Carol Lee @
212·505·9342

On the West Coast
520·708·9446

THE CAT LOVER'S BOOK OF FASCINATING FACTS

A Felicitous Look at Felines

ED LUCAIRE

SpeLling Works!

Fun-filled Reproducible Lessons and Mazes to Help Kids
Master Spelling Rules and Tackle Spelling Demons
by Jim Halverson

SMELLY Armor

Story by Joy Cowley
Illustrations by Rick Stromoski

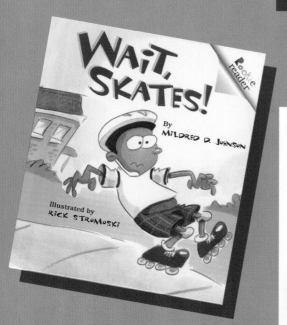

WAIT, SKATES!

By
Mildred D. Johnson

Rookie Reader

Illustrated by
Rick Stromoski

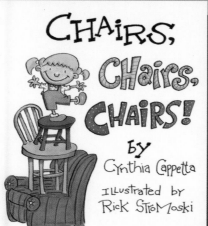

CHAIRS, CHAIRS, CHAIRS!

by
Cynthia Cappetta

ILLUSTRATED by
Rick Stromoski

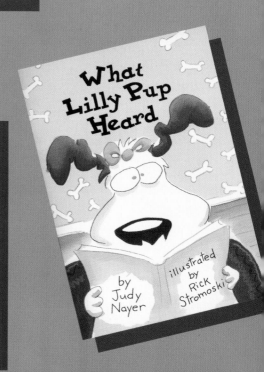

What Lilly Pup Heard

by
Judy Nayer

illustrated by Rick Stromoski

Magué
415 664 9541 www.mague.net/~mague

267

Ann Marie Rausch

21655 Hwy H

Monett , MO 65708

417. 235.7825

Leslie Newman

p: 206.622.3025
f: 206.622.3066

www.leslienewman.net
e: art@leslienewman.net

DANIEL CARLSON
2214 Williams Av. #2 • Cincinnati, OH 45212
513.531.3995 • Fax: 513.531.1054

JANE P. MILLER

831.684.1593

Sherry Neidigh
ILLUSTRATOR

2223 Preakness Court
Charlotte, NC 28273
704-587-7051

PARTIAL CLIENT LIST:
Highlights for Children
Harcourt Brace School Publisher
Great American Puzzle Factory
The Quarasan Group, Inc.
Frank Schaffer Publications
Kindermusik International Inc.
Ideal • Instructional Fair Publishing Group
Dog & Kennel
Cats & Kittens
The United Methodist Publishing House
Dalmatian Press

IMAGES FROM: BLACK AND WHITE, RISING MOON/NORTHLAND PUBLISHING

Joy Allen

Hannah Represents
(818) 378-1644

Partial List of Clients:
Bethany House
Dial Books for Young Readers
Grossett and Dunlap
Random House
Rising Moon
Waterbrook
Zondervan

ANN BARROW

REPRESENTED BY:
Christina A.Tugeau
110 Rising Ridge Rd
Ridgefield, CT 06877

203.438.7307
fax 203.894.1993
e-mail catartrep@aol.com
website: www.catugeau.com

Christina A.Tugeau • 203.438.7307

110 Rising Ridge Rd   Ridgefield, CT 06877

WINKY ADAM ▸ 370 CENTRAL PARK WEST ▸ NEW YORK, NY 10025 (212)423-0746

MICHEL STREFF
3735 South Berkley
Cincinnati, OH 45236
513.985.0568 phone/fax

LENA SHIFFMAN
69 Redwood Terrace
Flemington, N.J. 08822
(908) 782.6954   Fax: (908)782.6419
e-mail: lenas@ptd.net

408 353 9764 · www.flash.net/-odea · odea@flash.net

JOCK MACRAE
74 EAST LYNN AVE.,
TORONTO, ON.,
M4C 3X2
TEL. (416) 690-0401
EMAIL: jmacrae@istar.ca

IAN SOLOMON

My mommy once told me that I should never look too hard to try and find the meaning in something.....
She said that sometimes, when you find something that is full of beauty; that is everything it was ever meant to be.

DIGITAL ILLUSTRATION

JG

JERRY GONZALEZ

PHONE/FAX
(718) 204-8762

KATHLEEN KEMLY

206-782-8647

7543 - 13th NW • Seattle, WA 98117

Rosalind Charney Kaye

2517 Lincoln Street • Evanston, IL 60201
847.475.4161 • fax 847.475.5818 • e-mail: rosalind@kaye.com

Elizabeth

VICKI MORGAN & GA
MORGAN
GAYNIN
INC
194 THIRD AVE
NYC 10003
PH: (212) 475-0440 FX: (212) 353-8538

morgangaynin.com

Michele G. Katz

138 Cain Avenue
Braintree, MA 02184
781.843.1825

7958 Island Road
Eden Prairie MN 55347

952.975.0296 tele
952.975.0297 fax

Lynn@FellmanStudio.com
www.FellmanStudio.com

Fellman Studio Inc.
IMAGES for PRINT and SCREEN

RICHARD BERNAL   6 TEAK CT. ST. PETERS, MO 63376   636.922.0763

ciñdy cøuliñg
Illustrator

408.241.0675
www.couling.com

LAURA KNORR

335 GLENDALE AVENUE DECATUR GEORGIA 30030 USA

404.377.6623

Nora Koerber

626.791.1953

Fahimeh Amiri

661 Hammond Street • Chestnut Hill • MA • 02467

Tel/Fax: (617) 277 6011

The Monkey Bridge published by Knopf

Fahimeh Amiri

Marty Qatani
Grafix-n-Toons Studios
107 Rosewood Drive
Wappingers Falls, NY 12590
(845) 896-2021
www.martytoons.com
marty@martytoons.com

MICHAEL-CHÉ SWISHER

415.346.7113
http://home.earthlink.net/~michaelche/

Jazelle Lieske

Skyfeather Studio
Walnut Creek, CA
925.943.7163
www.skyfeather.com
Member SCBWI

Kevan Atteberry
illustration
p.o. box 40188
bellevue, wa 98015-4188
206/550-6353
kjatt@aol.com

D. Elizabeth Britton

29351 Smithville, OR 97378 • Tel/Fax 503.843.5055
illustration@ebritton.com • www.elizabethbritton.com

THE LONG WAY HOME

630·213·9003

www.portfolios.com/terrysirrell

ADD A
LITTLE CHARACTER
To Your STUFF!

How Many Pets?

Suzanne Beaky

RR 2 Box 84 • Greentop, MO 63546
660.665.4861 • e-mail:suzannebeaky@mac.com

Laura Jacobsen

208 E. Baseline Rd. #311
Tempe, AZ 85283
480.345.0217
laurartist@aol.com

Lynda Cohen

17094 Livorno Drive • Pacific Palisades, CA 90272

310.454.1273

Paula Lawson

972.414.4035
Fax: 972.530.7465
e-mail: paula@lawsoncomm.com

Dawn Fredericks

PHONE MAILBOX #: (626)299-8531
EMAIL: Snapdragons@hotmail.com

Michael Plank

(913) 631-7021 (phone/fax)
MPLANK9501@aol.com
5833 Monrovia
Shawnee, KS 66216-1913

Wendy Seese

illustrator

(310) 546-0086

Valerie Imhof

TEL 937.294.3582   FAX 937.294.1301   5350 Lindbergh Boulevard, Dayton, Ohio 45449

www.valerie-imhof.com

Gwen Connelly

312 943 4477

For more images see Picturebook
1998,1999,2000 and Blackbook 2001
email:gwen@certmag.com

Gwen Connelly
312 943 4477

For more images see Picturebook
1998,1999,2000 and Blackbook 2001
email:gwen@certmag.com

Edith Bingham, *Illustration*

482 South Street
Hollister, CA 95023
(831)636-8397
edithbing@yahoo.com

A Is for Salad

Mike Lester

New York Times Ten Best of 2000

"...stands ceremony on its ear..."
-Publishers Weekly
"The book is hilarious..."
-U.S. News & World Report
"...creates its own wonderful silliness."
-Booklist

mike Lester.com
706-234-7733

JESUS, JESUS EVERYWHERE

GO FISH!

Iris Van Rynbach

164 Keeney Street Glastonbury, CT 06033 • p.860.633.1239 • f. 860.652.8249
e-mail. IrisVan@aol.com

Bartt Warburton

11271 Ventura Blvd. Suite 298
Studio City, CA 91604
Phone: (818) 980-2226   Fax: (818) 980-2205   Email: PoeCrow@aol.com

Debra Wainwright
95 Carriage House Lane
Wrentham, Massachusetts 02093
phone/fax (508) 384-2759
e-mail: DebraWai@aol.com

For additional work see:
American Showcase 22 & 23

Deirdre Weinberg

201 Broderick Street
San Francisco, CA 94117
(415) 431-7725
DMMDEW@earthlink.net

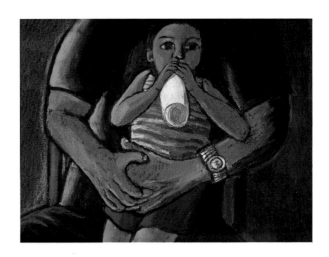

Jack Williams

P.O. Box 34464 Richmond, VA 23234 • 804.796.4797 phone/fax

RENAISSANCE HOUSE

http:www.renaissancehouse.net

¡HOLA!

Lopés - Watercolor

Ana Lopés - Watercolor

Victoria Escrivá - Watercolor and pencils

Petersen - Photoshop

Victoria Escrivá - Watercolor and pencils

Victoria Escrivá - Watercolor and pencils

Pablo Torrecilla - Water Color

Pablo Torrecilla - Acrylic

Torrecilla - Acrylic

Pablo Torrecilla - Acrylic

RENAISSANCE HOUSE

8907 Wilshire Blvd. Suite 102
Beverly Hills, CA 90211
Tel:310-358-5288   Fax:310-358-5282
http://www.renaissancehouse.net
e-mail: laredopub@cs.com

Denise Ortakales

509 Union Avenue• Laconia, NH 03246
603.528.2168 • www.ortakales.com • denise@ortakales.com

Herman Agency, inc.

Ronnie Ann Herman
350 Central Park West
New York, N.Y. 10025

tel: (212) 749-4907
fax: (212) 662-5151
e-mail: HermanAgen@aol.com
www.HermanAgencyInc.com

THIERRY COURTIN

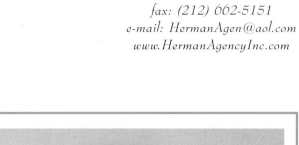

MARY BONO

GIDEON KENDALL

DOREEN GAY-KASSEL

Herman Agency, inc.

Ronnie Ann Herman
350 Central Park West
New York, N.Y. 10025

tel: (212) 749-4907
fax: (212) 662-5151
e-mail: HermanAgen@aol.com
www.HermanAgencyInc.com

MARK WEBER

BETINA OGDEN

JILL NEWTON

Herman Agency, inc.

Ronnie Ann Herman
350 Central Park West
New York, N.Y. 10025

tel: (212) 749-4907
fax: (212) 662-5151
e-mail: HermanAgen@aol.com
www.HermanAgencyInc.com

JOHN NEZ

TAMARA PETROSINO

NICK ZARIN-ACKERMAN

DOROTHY STOTT

Log onto www.HermanAgencyInc.com *to see more great art and artists.*

LINDA ROBERTS

4820 Thornwood Dr.
Acworth, GA 30102

770.591.5554
lrobertsatwork@mindspring.com

LIZ EDGE

205.967.1671
drewedge12@aol.com

Thomas Payne

The Penny & Stermer Group
ph 212.505.9342

www.pennystermergroup.com
e-mail: clstermer@aol.com

INDEX

Lodge, Katherine (187)
HK Portfolio
666 Greenwich Street Suite 860
New York NY 10014
p.212-675-5719 f.212-675-6341
harriet@hkportfolio.com
www.hkportfolio.com

Lohstoeter, Lori (210 & 211)
Lindgren & Smith
250 West 57th Street
New York NY 10107
p.212-397-7330 f.N/A
www.lindgrensmith.com

Lopes, Ana (319)
Renaissance House
8907 Willshire Blvd., Suite 102
Beverly Hills CA 90211
p.310-358-5288 f.310-358-5282
laredopub@cs.com
www.renaissancehouse.com

Lucas, Margeaux (187)
HK Portfolio
666 Greenwich Street Suite 860
New York NY 10014
p.212-675-5719 f.212-675-6341
harriet@hkportfolio.com
www.hkportfolio.com

Lustig, Loretta (262)
Carol Bancroft & Friends
121 Dodgingtown Road
Bethel CT 06801
p.203-748-4823 f.203-748-4581
artists@carolbancroft.com

Lyon, Tammie (77)
Laurie Lambert & Associates
9600 Stonemasters Drive
Loveland OH 45140
p.513-774-8777 f.513-774-8603
lalasc@aol.com
www.lambertassociatesinc.com

Macrae, Jock (280)
74 East Lynn Avenue
Toronto, ONT Canada M4C3X2
p.416-690-0401 f.N/A
jmacrae@istar.com

Madsen, Jim (199)
Shannon & Associates
333 West 57th Street, Suite 810
New York NY 10019
p.212-333-2551 f.212-333-2557
www.shannonassociates.com

Magnus, Erica (177)
15 Ondis Avenue
Athens OH 45701
p.740-593-7883 f.740-593-7883
emagnus@frognet.com

Magnuson, Diana (90)
Craven Design
234 Fifth Avenue
New York NY 10001
p.212-696-4680 f.212-532-2626
ts@cravendesignstudios.com

Magovern, Peg (24)
Ann Remen-Willis
2964 Colton Road
Pebble Beach CA 93953
p.831-655-1407 f.831-655-1408

Magué
(267)
545 Belvedere Street
San Francisco CA 94117
p.415-664-9541 f.415-989-5155
mague'@mague.com

Mahan, Benton (148)
Cornell & McCarthy LLC.
2-D Cross Highway
Westport CT 06880
p.203-454-4210 f.203-454-4258
cmartreps@aol.com

Majewski, Dawn (36)
3116 Addison Court
Bensalem PA 19020
p.215-752-4879 f.215-752-4879
dawnmajewski@earthlink.com

Malek, Kim (141)
Christine Prapas
12480 SE Wiese Road
Boring OR 97009
p.503-658-7070 f.503-658-3960
cprapas@teleport.com
www.christineprapas.com

Manders, John (187)
HK Portfolio
666 Greenwich Street Suite 860
New York NY 10014
p.212-675-5719 f.212-675-6341
harriet@hkportfolio.com
www.hkportfolio.com

Marino, Angelina (138)
Christine Prapas
12480 SE Wiese Road
Boring OR 97009
p.503-658-7070 f.503-658-3960
cprapas@teleport.com
www.christineprapas.com

Marino, Gianna (194)
467 Belvedere Street
San Francisco CA 94117
p.415-566-4707 f.415-566-4706
ginna@mindspring.com

Masheris, Bob (126)
Wilkinson Studios
901 West Jackson Blvd., Suite 201
Chicago IL 60607
p.312-226-0007 f.312-226-0404
www.wilkinsonstudios.com

Matskick, Anni (153)
Cornell & McCarthy LLC.
2-D Cross Highway
Westport CT 06880
p.203-454-4210 f.203-454-4258
cmartreps@aol.com

Mattern, Scott (263)
Carol Bancroft & Friends
121 Dodgingtown Road
Bethel CT 06801
p.203-748-4823 f.203-748-4581
artists@carolbancroft.com

Max, Louise (97)
PO Box 272
Jamaica VT 05343
p.802-297-2976 f.802-297-0090
takuskan@sover.com

Maydak, Mike (91)
Craven Design
234 Fifth Avenue
New York NY 10001
p.212-696-4680 f.212-532-2626
ts@cravendesignstudios.com

McCord, Kathi (51)
Bookmakers Ltd.
40 Mouse House Road PO Box
1086 Taos NM 87571
p.505-776-5434 f.505-776-2762
bookmakers@newmex.com

McDonald, Karen (6)
16 Fox Lane West
Painted Post NY 14870
p.607-936-3108 f.607-936-3108
karenmcd96@aol.com

McMahon, Bob (233)
240 South Third Street #O
Burbank CA 91502
p.818-955-8802 f.818-955-8802
bobtoons@earthlink.com

McNeil, Ted (54)
Bookmakers Ltd.
40 Mouse House Road PO Box
1086 Taos NM 87571
p.505-776-5434 f.505-776-2762
bookmakers@newmex.com

Meisel, Paul (187)
HK Portfolio
666 Greenwich Street Suite 860
New York NY 10014
p.212-675-5719 f.212-675-6341
harriet@hkportfolio.com
www.hkportfolio.com

Mendenhall, Cheryl (158)
Cornell & McCarthy LLC.
2-D Cross Highway
Westport CT 06880
p.203-454-4210 f.203-454-4258
cmartreps@aol.com

Merer, Laura (79)
Laurie Lambert & Associates
9600 Stonemasters Drive
Loveland OH 45140
p.513-774-8777 f.513-774-8603
lalasc@aol.com
www.lambertassociatesinc.com

Micthell, Judith (55)
Bookmakers Ltd.
40 Mouse House Road PO Box
1086 Taos NM 87571
p.505-776-5434 f.505-776-2762
bookmakers@newmex.com

Miller, Jane (271)
1260 Day Valley Road
Aptos CA 95003
p.831-684-1593 f.N/A
janieann@cruzio.com

Minor, Wendell (99)
15 Old North Road PO Box 1135
Washington CT 06793
p.860-868-9101 f.860-868-9512
wendell@minorart.com

Miyake, Yoshie (262)
Carol Bancroft & Friends
121 Dodgingtown Road
Bethel CT 06801
p.203-748-4823 f.203-748-4581
artists@carolbancroft.com

Miyamoto, Mas (175)
Square Moon
6 Montery Terrace
Orinda CA 94563
p.925-253-9451 f.925-253-9452
info@sqmoon.com

Mongeau, Marc (107)
Marlena Agency
145 Witherspoon Street
Princeton NJ 8542
p.609-252-9405 f.609-252-1949
marzena@bellatlantic.net, marlenaagency.com

Monks, Julie (188)
HK Portfolio
666 Greenwich Street Suite 860
New York NY 10014
p.212-675-5719 f.212-675-6341
harriet@hkportfolio.com
www.hkportfolio.com

Moore, Harry (169)
Deborah Wolfe Ltd.
731 North 24th Street
Philadelphia PA 19130
p.215-232-6666 f.215-232-6585
www.deborahwolfeltd.com

Moore, Cyd (30 & 31)
32240 Verona Circle
Beverly Hills MI 48025
p.248-723-0847 f.248-723-0914
cyd@cydmoore.com

Morrison, Cathy (144)
6209 South Gespe Court
Littleton CO 80121
p.720-493-1954 f.N/A
bigchief10@aol.com